Series 606B

A Ladybird 'Easy-Reading' book

'People at Work'

THE ROAD MAKERS

by I. & J. HAVENHAND
with illustrations by JOHN BERRY

Publishers WILLS & HEPWORTH Ltd Loughborough
First published 1967 © *Printed in England*

THE ROAD MAKERS

Thousands of years ago, our country was covered by forests and swamps. There were no roads, only tracks made by animals and the men who hunted them.

When people settled in small villages, they made tracks from one village to another so that they could trade with each other. At first these tracks were just hard earth.

As more trading was done and pack-horses were used, the tracks were made better.

7214 0073 6

When the Romans came they needed good roads to help their soldiers to move safely and quickly around our country.

To mark out where to build a road, the Romans lit bonfires a long way from each other. The soldiers and slave workers made the road in a straight line from fire to fire.

They made their roads with layers of large and small stones. Sometimes the top was made with large, flat stones set as wide apart as the chariot wheels, with smaller stones in between.

We can still see parts of Roman roads to-day.

After the Romans left Britain, the roads were not mended. No new roads were made until about 1640 when stage coaches began to be used to carry people and mail. The roads were so bad that often the stage coaches tipped over and people were injured.

Later, the Government let groups of people make roads. These roads were called 'turnpike' roads. They had gates on them and travellers had to pay to use the roads.

Many turnpike roads were not well made until two engineers called Telford and Macadam worked out how to make good roads.

Telford's roads were very solid with large stones for the foundation and smaller ones on top.

Macadam's roads were not as solid as Telford's. They had no large stones for a foundation. Smaller stones were put in layers and the top was finished with broken stone and grit. These roads wore well with horse-drawn traffic.

When cars started to use the roads they quickly wore away the top. To make the roads wear better, tar was mixed with small stones and used for the top layer. This was called 'tarmacadam'.

As more cars and lorries used the roads, the Government saw that new and even better roads would have to be made.

The person in charge of all main roads is called the Minister of Transport.

Before new roads are started, the Minister asks men to find out where roads are most needed. These men take a traffic count or census. This is done by making check-points at places near to where new roads may be made. Drivers are asked where they are going and from where they have come.

Sometimes traffic is counted by an automatic counter. A black rubber pipe is fixed to the road. The mechanism in the box counts each car or lorry as it passes over the pipe.

If the Minister of Transport decides that a new road is needed, he asks his road engineers to work out a route.

The engineers examine all the possible routes. They try to find one that will by-pass towns. The engineers try to go round land that is very hilly and they look for the easiest places to cross rivers.

The best route is chosen and a more careful survey is made. Plans of all parts of the road are drawn.

Engineers bore holes every few hundred yards to see what the ground is like where the road will be. Samples of earth are tested to see if concrete will be spoiled by it. The engineers also have to make sure that the ground is not too soft to carry the weight of the bridges.

The land over which the road will run is bought and the centre line of the road is pegged out.

Draughtsmen who make drawings, help consulting engineers to design the new road. Bridges on and over the road have to be designed and the layout of junctions planned. Service stations, where motorists can stop for petrol or a meal, are designed.

After the drawings have been made, quantity surveyors decide how much material, such as stone and concrete, will be needed.

Large road construction firms are then asked to give a 'tender' for building the road. The tender is the price they will charge.

Men who work for the construction firm that is chosen to make the road, make their plans of how the work is to be done.

The construction engineers decide which bridges need to be built first. These bridges are the ones that will be most useful to the workmen.

At several places along the route, huts are built as offices, kitchens, canteens and stores. Fuel tanks are built to store the petrol and oil for the lorries and machines. Some of the men live on these sites. They live in large caravans.

A lot of different and expensive machines are used to build a road. The engineers must arrange to have these machines at the right places and see that they are kept in good working order. Sometimes they hire the machines from other firms or pay the firms to do the work.

Large numbers of men are needed. Some of the men always work for the construction firm and in any part of the country. Other men only work on the road if they can travel to it each day. The construction firm uses its own lorries and buses to carry these men to and from work.

The first job that the men must do is to clear the route. There may be buildings in the way that have to be knocked down. This is easily done by bulldozers.

The route may pass through wooded country. Workmen cut down the trees. The roots are dug out and dragged away by tractors. Hedges are ripped out and burned.

When the clearing is done the job of levelling begins. The topsoil is scraped off by large machines. This soil is saved and used again later as topsoil, perhaps for grass verges.

RTP
6

The scrapers are like large boxes and they are dragged along by tractors. They cut off layers of earth and carry it away.

After the topsoil has been moved, the men begin the work of getting to the level where the road will be. Millions of tons of earth have to be moved by the different machines.

Men using mechanical diggers dig away the ground. They use bulldozers to push the earth. Mechanical shovels lift the spare soil into dumper trucks and tip-lorries to be taken away.

Sometimes cuttings have to be made through hills. The engineers use the earth from the cuttings to build up embankments where the ground is low. This is called 'cut and fill.'

Small tunnels for streams and farm tracks are built first. The soil is then laid over them and rolled until it is firm.

The engineers plan the work so that as much earth-moving as possible is done in the drier, summer months. To drain away water, ditches are dug along the sides of the route.

The workmen seal the ground with a thin layer of tar to stop it becoming soaked by rain. After this, the edges of the road are built up with concrete. The foundations of the road are put inside the edges.

The engineers will have decided whether to build a solid road like Telford's or a softer road like Macadam's.

To-day, solid roads are made of layers of concrete. Thousands of tons of concrete are used for every mile of road. Special concrete mixing plants are set up along the route.

The first layer of a concrete road is made of 'lean' concrete. This is made of sand and stones and does not have much cement and water in it.

Fleets of lorries carry the concrete from the mixing plants to where the men need it. The men tip the concrete into a machine called a 'paver'.

The paver is moved slowly along. As it moves it spreads the concrete evenly over a wide stretch of road. The lean concrete is then rolled to make it firm.

Men cover the lean concrete with polythene sheeting to separate it from the next layer.

The top layer of the road is made of reinforced concrete. Thick steel netting is put over the poly-thene, and concrete is spread over it. Men use another machine, called a 'vibrator', to make the concrete firm. The vibrator has a rod which shakes. This rod is pushed into the wet concrete to pack it around the reinforcement netting.

A machine with a long arm that moves backwards and forwards, smooths off the top of the road.

On some kinds of ground the engineers decide to make the road of asphalt. At one time tarmac was used. The tar was made at gas works. To-day, bitumen is used and this comes from oil. A mixture of very small stones and bitumen is called asphalt. A lot of asphalt that is used comes from Trinidad where there is a huge asphalt lake.

To heat the asphalt that will be used, large mixing plants are built along the route. These are usually built near to quarries that will supply the stones.

Asphalt roads have foundations of either large, tarred stones or lean concrete. On top of this a layer of smaller, tarred stones is laid. The roads then have one or two thick layers of hot, rolled asphalt.

Lorry drivers from the asphalt plants tip their loads into a machine. The machine keeps the asphalt hot and spreads it as it moves along. The asphalt is rolled firm by men driving motor rollers.

A thin layer of very good asphalt is put on top as a wearing surface.

As different parts of the road are finished they join up to make a continuous road. Most new roads to-day are motorways.

A large part of the work on motorways is the making of bridges. Some bridges are made in the very early stages and others are made while the roadwork is going on. Bridges have to be made to carry the motorway over other roads and railways or under them. Rivers have to be crossed and deep valleys spanned.

To-day, most bridges are made of concrete. Sometimes concrete beams are made at factories and fitted together on the site of the bridge. Other bridges are made on the site by pouring concrete into moulds or wooden shuttering made into the shape of the bridge. When the concrete is dry, the shuttering is taken away.

Very long bridges are built to carry roads across valleys. These are called viaducts.

The engineers try to make all bridges pleasant to look at as well as strong.

While the road is being built, some men are working on the sites of the service stations.

Service stations are the only places on motorways where drivers are allowed to stop. These stations are built about every twenty-five miles.

Slip roads are built from the motorway to the two parts of the service station. A bridge across the road joins them. Kitchens, dining rooms, washrooms and toilets are built. A shop and petrol pumps are made. There is even a place where people can have picnics.

Vehicles can only join or leave motorways at special junctions. The engineers try to have as few junctions as possible. These have to be carefully planned and are often very large.

Roads pass under or over the motorway so that no vehicles have to cross the very fast moving traffic.

The wide stretch of grass up the middle of motorways is to keep apart fast moving vehicles that are travelling in opposite directions. Some motorways have two traffic lanes each way and some have three lanes.

When the motorway is nearly ready for use, men paint the white lines for the traffic lanes. Other workmen put up sign boards. These are very large so that they can be easily read by drivers. The signs tell the drivers the names of towns or when they are near a service station.

Some signs are put up to warn drivers of danger such as fog, snow or accident. These signs are switched on by the police.

Telephones are put at the roadside for drivers to call for help if they break down.

TA 110
SOS
7312 PP

Men who work for the Ministry of Transport have to think about traffic in towns as well as on the motorways. Better roads are needed in towns to keep traffic moving.

At busy cross-roads, underpasses and overpasses are being made. These let traffic pass under and over the cross-roads without stopping.

It is difficult to build wide roads in towns. In future, fast town roads may have to be built on two levels. The traffic will travel one way at ground level and the opposite way on a road built above it like a bridge.

SOME OF THE NEW BRITISH

Selected by permission from The New Traffic Signs (HMSO)

Warning signs

Cross roads

Roundabout

Double bend

Two way traffic straight ahead

Pedestrian crossing

Road works

Slippery roads

Level crossing without gate or barrier ahead

Dual carriage way ends

Children

Horses or ponies

Falling rocks